A PARRAGON BOOK

Published by Parragon Book Service Ltd,
Units 13-17, Avonbridge Trading Estate, Atlantic Road,
Avonmouth, Bristol BS11 9QD

Produced by The Templar Company plc,
Pippbrook Mill, London Road, Dorking, Surrey RH4 1JE

Edited by Caroline Repchuk
Designed by Mark Summersby

Printed and bound in Great Britain

ISBN 0 75250 792 3

FAIRY TALE LAND

Written by Caroline Repchuk
Illustrated by Maggie Downer

‖ •PARRAGON• ‖

Welcome to Fairy Tale Land

You have entered a land filled with magic and enchantment - the wonderful world of Fairy Tales! As you turn the pages some of your favourite fairy tales will spring to life. Look at each picture and you will spot all sorts of familiar characters. You'll find a list of things to discover on each spread, some of which will be harder to find than others. Try making your own list, too, of all the extra characters and objects from the stories that you find. And don't forget that, lurking on every spread is the Big Bad Wolf. He loves to sneak about and hide. See if you can find him on all the pages, but watch out! Sometimes he'll appear in disguise! Happy searching!

Cinderella

When the Fairy Godmother sends Cinderella to the Prince's ball in a beautiful glass coach, even her ugly sisters don't recognise her. But as she runs away into the night, she leaves a clue to her identity behind! Can you find what it is, and can you also find these other objects which feature in the story:

- **Four lizards**
- **A fat rat**
- **A magic wand**
- **A pumpkin**

Rapunzel

Since being stolen as a baby by an evil witch, Rapunzel
has grown up shut away in a tower. Now a handsome
Prince has come to save her, but the witch has other
plans! Can you spot what the witch will use to keep the
Prince from reaching Rapunzel? Can you also find:

- **The Prince's horse**
- **The witch's cottage**
- **The witch's cat**
- **Four songbirds**

The Little Mermaid

The Little Mermaid longs to become human so she can marry the Prince that she saved in a storm. She has made a terrible bargain with the Sea Witch. In return for a potion which will make her grow legs, she has given the witch something very precious - her tongue. Can you see where the witch has put it ? And can you also find some of the lovely things in this underwater world:

- **Her five mermaid sisters**
- **Four jolly crabs**
- **Ten red fish**
- **Six seahorses**

Beauty and the Beast

When a handsome Prince is turned into an ugly beast by a wicked witch, he is sad and lonely because he no longer has any friends. Everyone is afraid of him. But then kind Beauty meets him, and fills his life with love. Can you see what he has given her as a present, and can you find these other objects that are part of the story:

- **A dozen perfect red roses**
- **A magic gold ring**
- **The wicked witch**
- **A handkerchief**

Hansel and Grettel

Poor Hansel and Grettel have been left alone in the woods by their parents, and they cannot find their way home. Instead they have found their way to a rather tasty little house. But they should look out, because can you see who lives there? And can you find these other things that are part of the story:

- **Ten white pebbles**
- **A white dove**
- **An axe**
- **Five bones**

The Frog Prince

The young Princess has made a promise to a frog, which she is horrified to find she has to keep! In return for finding her golden ball, he now expects to eat from her golden plate, drink from her goblet and sleep on her pillow. Can you see what he has brought the Princess as a present from the pond? Can you also spot these things :

- **The golden ball**
- **The feather pillow**
- **The golden plate**
- **The goblet**

Snow White

Snow White has fled deep into the forest, after discovering her wicked stepmother's evil plan to kill her. She is staying in a little cottage with seven kind dwarfs, who work in a diamond mine, where she will be safe — or will she? Can you guess who is coming through the forest to tempt her with a poisoned apple? And can you find these things from the story:

- **The magic mirror**
- **The huntsman**
- **Six diamonds**
- **The poisoned apple**
- **The seven dwarfs**
- **The Prince**

Puss in Boots

Clever Puss in Boots has devised a cunning plan to take
his master from rags to riches. So far his plan has been
successful, and the King is most impressed with the
handsome boy's gifts and his vast lands. Now Puss has
won his master a castle from a fearsome ogre, by getting
the ogre to change himself into something else. Can you
guess what it is, and can you guess what Puss must do to
keep the ogre from returning? Now look for these things
from the story:

- **Three rabbits**
- **Two pheasants**
- **A farmer**
- **A lion**

Little Red Riding Hood

Little Red Riding Hood has no idea of the surprise that's in store for her when she goes to visit her sick Grandma with a basketful of cakes. "What big eyes you have Grandma," she says. She soon finds out that's not all that 'Grandma's' got! Can you find where her Grandma really is, and can you find:

- **A basket of cakes**
- **The woodchopper**
- **Grandma's slippers**
- **Grandma's cat**

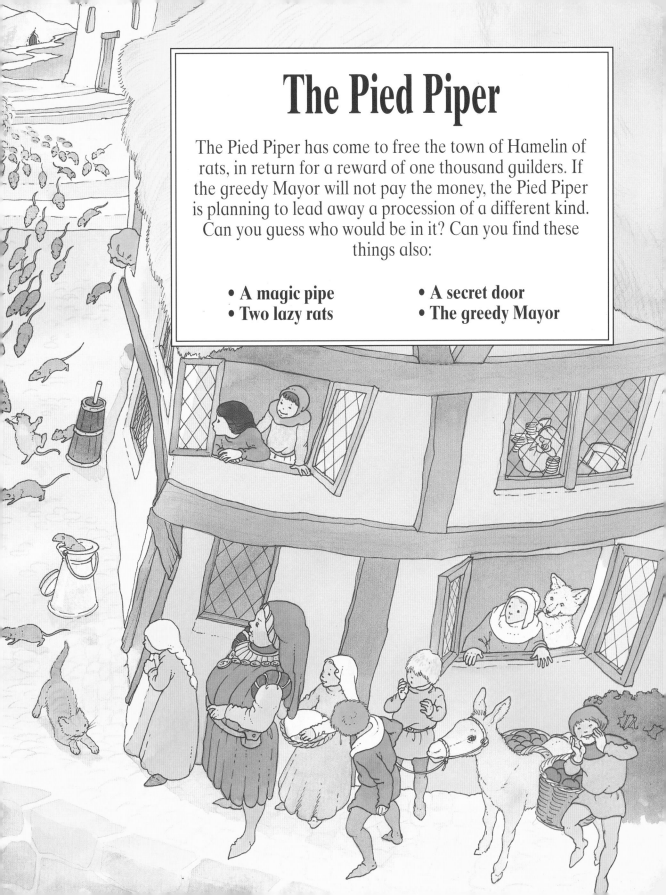

The Pied Piper

The Pied Piper has come to free the town of Hamelin of rats, in return for a reward of one thousand guilders. If the greedy Mayor will not pay the money, the Pied Piper is planning to lead away a procession of a different kind. Can you guess who would be in it? Can you find these things also:

- **A magic pipe**
- **Two lazy rats**
- **A secret door**
- **The greedy Mayor**

The Emperor's New Clothes

Two smart young tailors have come to town, and persuaded the King to pay them bags of gold for a splendid new suit to wear in his grand procession. But as he parades along, a small boy in the crowd spots something amiss. Can you spot what it is, or are you altogether as crazy as the King? Now find these things too:

- **The clever boy**
- **The crafty tailors**
- **A pair of scissors**
- **Some bags of gold**